iScience
Science in the Real World

Measurement

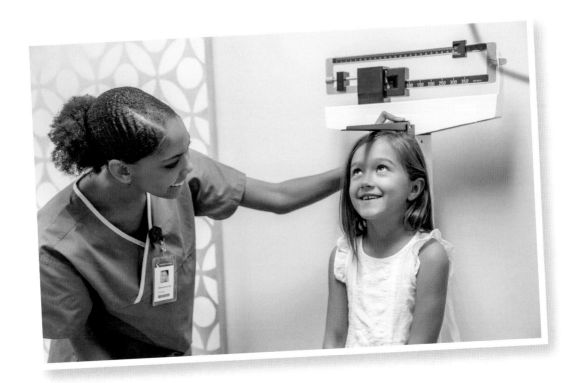

by Emily Sohn and Karen J. Rothbardt

NORWOOD HOUSE PRESS
Chicago, Illinois

Norwood House Press
Chicago, Illinois
For information regarding Norwood House Press, please visit our website at
www.norwoodhousepress.com or call 866-565-2900.

Contributors: Edward Rock, Project Content Consultant
Editor: Lauren Dupuis-Perez
Designer: Sara Radka
Fact Checker: Sam Rhodes

Photo Credits in this revised edition include: Getty Images: Blend Images, cover, 1, Hero
Images, 4, iStockphoto, 17; Pixabay: Byunilho background, (paper texture), GDJ, background
(tech pattern); Shutterstock: Muellek Josef, 20, PJjaruwan, 28; Wikimedia: Matthew Harris
Jouett, 27

Library of Congress Cataloging-in-Publication Data
Names: Sohn, Emily, author. | Rothbardt, Karen, author. | Sohn, Emily. iScience.
Title: Measurement / by Emily Sohn and Karen J. Rothbardt.
Description: [2019 edition]. | Chicago, Illinois : Norwood House Press, [2019] |
    Series: iScience | Audience: Ages 8-10. Includes bibliographical references and index.
Identifiers: LCCN 2018057944 | ISBN 9781684509591 (hardcover) | ISBN
    9781684043828 (pbk.) | ISBN 9781684043934 (ebook)
Subjects: LCSH: Measurement—Juvenile literature. |
    Units of measurement—Juvenile literature.
Classification: LCC QC90.6 .S64 2019 | DDC 530.8—dc23
LC record available at https://lccn.loc.gov/2018057944

Hardcover ISBN: 978-1-68450-959-1
Paperback ISBN: 978-1-68404-382-8

Contents

Note to Caregivers:
In this updated and revised iScience series, each book poses many questions to the reader. Some are open ended and ask what the reader thinks. Discuss these questions with your child and guide him or her in thinking through the possible answers and outcomes. There are also questions posed which have a specific answer. Encourage your child to read through the text to determine the correct answer. Most importantly, throughout the book, encourage answers using critical thinking skills and imagination. In the back of the book you will find answers to these questions, along with additional resources to help support you as you share the book with your child.

Words that are **bolded** are defined in the glossary in the back of the book.

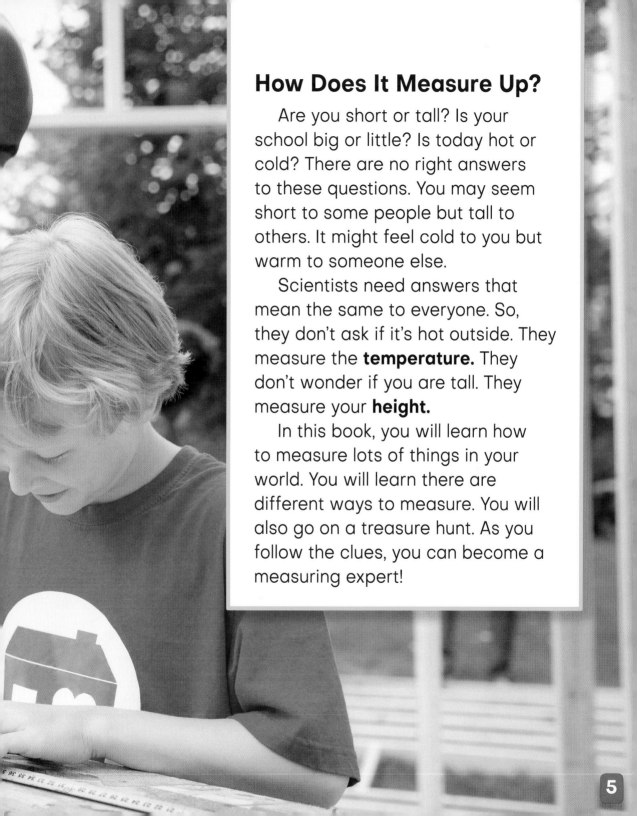

How Does It Measure Up?

Are you short or tall? Is your school big or little? Is today hot or cold? There are no right answers to these questions. You may seem short to some people but tall to others. It might feel cold to you but warm to someone else.

Scientists need answers that mean the same to everyone. So, they don't ask if it's hot outside. They measure the **temperature.** They don't wonder if you are tall. They measure your **height.**

In this book, you will learn how to measure lots of things in your world. You will learn there are different ways to measure. You will also go on a treasure hunt. As you follow the clues, you can become a measuring expert!

Treasure Hunt

It's your birthday! One of your presents is hidden. To find it, you must follow a series of clues on pieces of paper.

Here is your first clue: "Look 50 centimeters (cm) to the left of your favorite chair. Hint: 50 cm is about the average **length** of a house cat." You look a cat's length to the left of the chair. There, you find your next clue.

The second clue reads: "Find an object that is full of food. Look at a spot 10 inches (in) up from the ground." You run to the refrigerator. You look down near your knees. The note is your next clue!

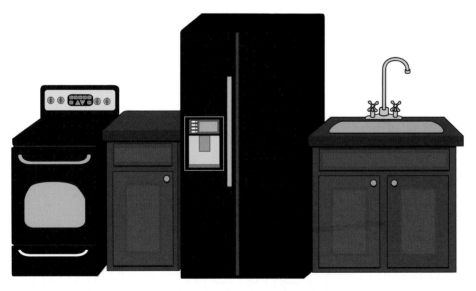

One of these objects is full of food. Is your clue there?

You needed a hint that 50 cm is about the length of a cat. But you somehow knew that 10 in is somewhere between the floor and your knees. How did you know? You've probably used a 12-in ruler many times, so you knew about how high 10 in is.

Here's your next clue. Remember it. You'll need it in a few pages.

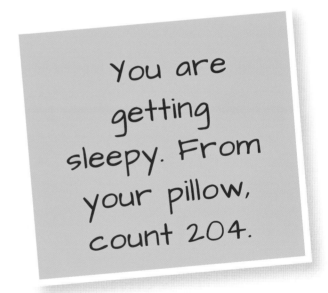

You are getting sleepy. From your pillow, count 204.

What does all this mean? Keep reading. You will learn more about measurements. And everything you learn will bring you closer to your present!

Discover Activity

Materials

- ruler
- pencil
- piece of paper
- book

Measure It!

In the treasure hunt, you found your clues in clever ways. For example, you knew the average length of a house cat. That helped you make a good guess of how far from your chair you should look for your second clue. Guesses like that are called **estimates**.

Find a ruler, a pencil, a piece of paper, and a book. On the paper, draw a chart like this:

Object	Estimated Length	Actual Length
pencil		
paper		
book		

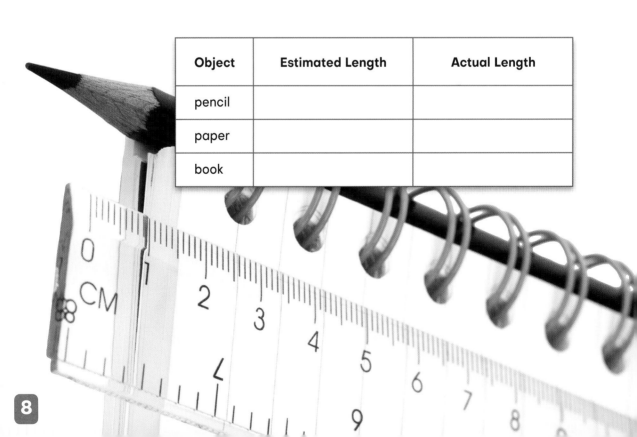

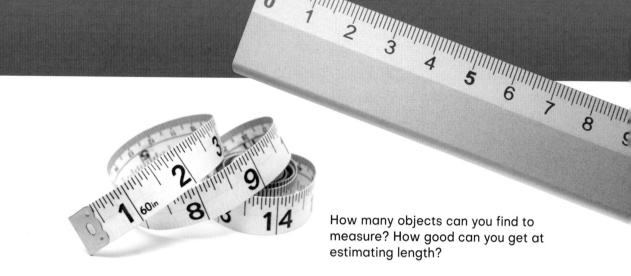

How many objects can you find to measure? How good can you get at estimating length?

Estimate the length of each object. Write your guess in the "estimate" column. Then, use the ruler to measure the object. How close was your guess to the actual length? Did you measure in centimeters or inches? Now, try more objects. You can add new rows for leaves, crayons, and other things. Do your guesses get better after a while?

Hmmm.
I think my hand is about 5 in.

Tools of the Trade

Guessing can take you only so far. Say you want to know the exact length of an object. Grab a tool. For small things, use a ruler. A meterstick is longer so it works for measuring bigger things. A tape measure reaches even farther.

As you read on, you'll learn of tools used to measure things other than length.

How Do Scientists Measure Length?

You might use the words *long* and *short* to describe length. Scientists need to be more **precise**. They might measure a snake's length one week and again the next week. The difference tells them exactly how much the snake grew. Saying the snake is *longer* isn't very helpful. But saying the snake is *2.8 in longer* is helpful.

Two Languages of Measurement

In Spain, people speak Spanish. In France, people speak French. In science, people talk with numbers. The most common way to measure in science is with the **metric system.** Another way to measure is with the **US customary system**. Both use their own standard **units.** Units describe how big, far away, heavy, hot, loud, or bright things are.

How would you measure a snake's growth?

Units are like blocks that lock together. Small ones add up to make bigger ones. A tiny block for length in the metric system is a millimeter (mm). Put 10 mm together and you get 1 centimeter (cm). A **meter (m)** is made up of 100 cm. A thousand m make a kilometer (km). 1 m is the same as 39.37 inches (in). That's a little more than 3 feet (ft). 3 ft is also called a yard (yd). To go back and forth between systems is called making conversions.

US Customary System	Metric System	Conversions
1 foot = 12 inches	1 millimeter = 1/1,000 meter	1 inch = 2.54 centimeters
1 yard = 3 feet	1 centimeter = 1/100 meter	1 yard = 0.914 meter
1 mile = 1,760 yards	1 kilometer = 1,000 meters	1 mile = 1.609 kilometer

measurement conversions

In science, it is very important to label units. Say you ordered a new bike. You assumed that the measurement of 44 meant inches. However, it meant centimeters. Only a doll could fit on such a tiny bike!

Why Metric?

In the United States, inches, feet, yards, and miles are used to measure distance. These units show up on street signs and in sports games. But scientists like the metric system. Math is easier with metric units. Look at these problems:

You are going to run 6.5 miles. How many feet is that?
There are 5,280 feet in a mile.
What is $6.5 \times 5,280$?
34,320 feet

You are going to run 6.5 kilometers. How many meters is that?
There are 1,000 meters in a kilometer.
What is $6.5 \times 1,000$?
6,500 meters

It doesn't say so, but this sign uses miles to measure distance.

Our brains like the numbers 10, 100, and 1,000. Many people can multiply by these numbers in their heads. Can you see how easy it was to come up with 6,500? It wasn't easy at all to come up with 34,320. Most of us need pencils to multiply by 5,280.

Numbers Without Words

Now back to the treasure hunt. Remember the note you found at the bottom of the refrigerator? Go where it would logically take you—to your bedroom. Look at the clue. It says to count from the pillow to 204. But 204 what? You get up and grab a tape measure. From the pillow, your room is 132 in long. That's 335 cm and 3,352.8 mm. The room is 120 in wide. That's 305 cm. The number 204 can't describe the length or **width** of your room.

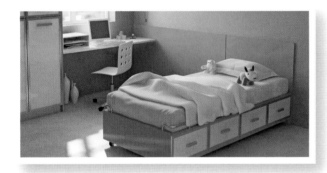

How far is your pillow from the floor?

Wait a minute! You stand on your bed and hold up the tape measure. It is 204 cm from your pillow to the ceiling. The number describes the height of your room from your pillow to the ceiling. On the ceiling, you find a new clue. It says 0°. Huh?

Don't worry. We'll come back to this. You won't be left wondering for long!

Time Keeps On Ticking

How much time have you spent reading this book? How about this sentence? You could guess. Or you could measure using a stopwatch. To track time, we use seconds, minutes, hours, days, weeks, months, years, and so on for the units. It takes about 1 second to say "one thousand." There are 60 seconds in a minute. There are 60 minutes in an hour. There are 24 hours in a day. There are 365 days in most years.

What other activities can you think of that you can measure with a stopwatch?

A second may seem like a tiny blip of time. But scientists often count in milliseconds. There are 1,000 milliseconds in 1 second.

How long does it take you to read this page? Can you answer in more than one way? Don't forget to use units.

The Need for Speed

You are racing to solve the treasure hunt. You read each note as fast as you can. You run from clue to clue. You feel as fast as the wind. But how fast are you really going? To measure speed, you need to track both length and time. Street signs in the United States use miles per hour (mph). Other countries use kilometers per hour (kph). Many US highways have speed limits of about 60 mph.

This New Zealand speed limit sign is recommending 55 kph for the winding road ahead.

At that speed, a car goes 60 miles in 1 hour. You can also track speed in meters per second. Or you could use inches per minute. It all depends on what you are trying to measure. How fast do you think you can run?

Did You Know?

The fastest car in history was called Thrust SSC. The car traveled 1 mile in 4.7 seconds. That's 763 miles (1,228 km) per hour. At that speed, the British could cross their entire country in less than an hour!

How Do Scientists Measure Mass and Weight?

When you step on a bathroom scale, you measure your **weight.** Scientists also talk about **mass.** Many people confuse the two. But they are really quite different.

Mass vs. Weight

Mass measures how much matter, or material, is in an object. You are made up of a certain amount of mass. It doesn't change from place to place no matter where you are. But weight measures the pull of **gravity** on your body. And the pull of gravity can change. The Moon has less gravity than Earth has. When gravity changes, weight does, too. On the Moon, objects weigh about 1/6 as much, or about 17% as much, as they do here on Earth. Say you weigh 100 pounds on Earth. About how much would you weigh on the Moon?

Objects and people weigh less on the Moon than they weigh on Earth.

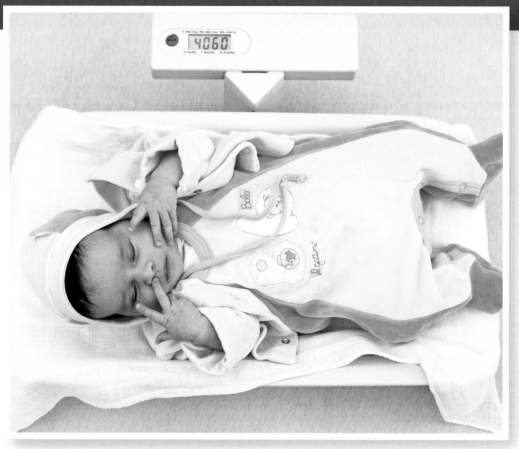

At more than 4 kilograms, this baby is a bit bigger than the average newborn!

Adding Up

To weigh things, scientists use grams as a basic unit. One thousand milligrams (mg) make up 1 gram (g). Medicine often gets measured in milligrams. One thousand grams make up 1 kilogram (kg). Most newborn babies weigh about 3 kg. These units are all part of the metric system.

More or Less of You

Step on a scale. Write down how much you weigh. (Do you know the US customary unit for weight?) Now, find out how much you would weigh elsewhere in the solar system. Use the chart below. Remember to mark your units.

Place in Space	Multiply Your Weight by	Your Weight
Mars	0.3	
Jupiter	2.5	
The Sun	27	
Venus	0.9	

Use a chart like this to record what your weight would be on different planets in the solar system.

Compounding Pharmacist

You have probably seen a pharmacist at the drugstore counting out tiny tablets behind the pharmacy counter. Pharmacists can also mix special medications based on a patient's needs. This is called compounding.

Pharmacists study for four years after college to learn chemistry and compounding before receiving their certification to work.

All pharmacists are trained in compounding in pharmacy school. They learn to crush tablets, add flavoring, change the form of a medication, and even remove ingredients, like gluten. Pharmacists must know all of the correct measurements to create the exact medication needed. Some pharmacies have complex labs for changing medications. Pharmacists use special tools for compounding, like a mortar and pestle, cylinders, weights, and tiny spatulas.

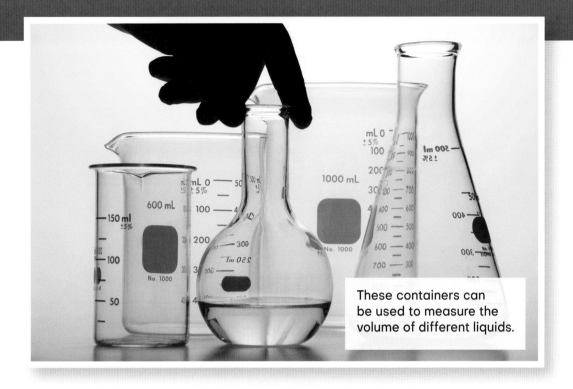

These containers can be used to measure the volume of different liquids.

What Are Some Different Ways to Measure Volume?

Now think about that clue: 0°. As you wander around the house wondering what it might mean, you come to the kitchen again. You notice tall, skinny cups. You see wide, round bowls.

The amount of space an object takes up is its **volume**. That's how much space is inside. Say you want to measure the volume of an object. First, you need to know how tall, long, and wide the object is. Why might you want to measure volume?

How Much Stuff?

You have a box 20 cm long. It is 6 cm wide. And it is 30 cm high. To get volume, multiply length by width by height. The final unit will be cubic centimeters (cm³). You might also see cubic meters (m³) sometimes.

30 cm

6 cm

20 cm

Length × Width × Height = Volume
20 cm × 6 cm × 30 cm = Box Volume

What is the volume of the box? Is your surprise present in there? No. Volume doesn't match the 0° clue.

Odd Shapes

You can also find the volumes of things with strange shapes. The container below has numbers and lines on it. They show how many milliliters (mL) of water are inside. Place an object of any shape into the water. Be sure it doesn't float. You will see the water rise. The amount that the water rises shows the volume of the object you put into the water. The amount that the water rises is called displacement. The object displaced the water so the water level rose.

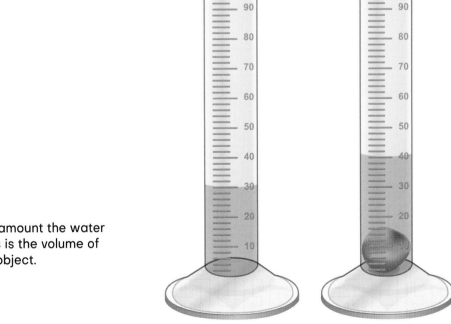

The amount the water rises is the volume of the object.

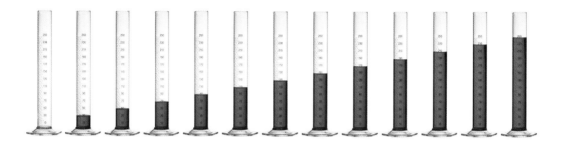

Containers of the same size can measure many different amounts of volume.

Pssst! Want to learn a trick? One mL of water weighs 1 gram (g). A liter (L) equals 1,000 mL. That means that 1 L of water weighs 1,000 g. That's 1 kg. Voilà! It's an easy way to find the weight of water.

But here's a twist. Not all liquids weigh the same. Salt water is heavier than tap water. Milk is heavier than water, too. Whole milk is heavier than skim.

What Units Are Used to Measure Temperature?

You're in the kitchen. You look at the last clue. It says 0°. It must be about temperature. Temperature tells you how hot something is. The metric unit for temperature is degrees Celsius (°C). The US customary system uses degrees Fahrenheit (°F).

How Do Celsius and Fahrenheit Compare?

Water typically freezes at 0°C. That's the same as 32°F. At sea level, water boils at 100°C, or 212°F. This **thermometer** shows both scales.

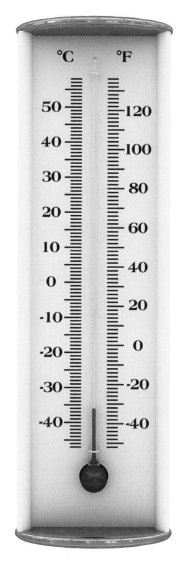

What's the temperature in Celsius for 80° Fahrenheit?

When you have a fever, your body is fighting disease.

Body Heat

Have you ever had a fever? Your body likes to stay at about 37°C. That's 98.6°F. A fever is when your body temperature goes up. The temperature may reach 102°F or higher. It feels awful to be that sick. It is best just to rest, drink water, and let the fever do its work. A fever helps to fight disease by making it harder for germs to live and reproduce.

Thomas Jefferson and the History of US Measurement

The year was 1790. The US had just won its independence from England. President George Washington gave Secretary of State Thomas Jefferson an important job. He told Jefferson to make rules about measurements, weights, and money for the whole country. Each state had its own system. Washington wanted the whole country to use the same system. This was especially important for buying, selling, and trading. Jefferson came up with a decimal system because

Thomas Jefferson was the third US president.

he believed everyone could understand it. Although the US Customary System we use today is different from Jefferson's first proposal, we still use his rules for identifying and counting money today.

Most freezers are kept at 0°F or below.

You're still looking at your last clue: 0°. But what are the units? 0°C would be cold, but not that cold. Water typically freezes right at 0°C. You don't see any slushy ice anywhere. But, wait. Ice makes you think of something! 0°F is the perfect temperature for a kitchen freezer. You open the freezer door. On the top shelf sits your favorite kind of ice cream. There is a bow on it. Happy birthday! You measured your way to your gift!

Beyond the Puzzle

In this book, you learned about length, width, and weight. You explored volume, weight, mass, and temperature. You also learned the value of units.

Now it's your turn. Hide a present for someone. Give a series of clues to get them to it. Include as many types of measurement as you can in the clues. You can offer help if needed. After all, you're the expert now!

Glossary

estimates: reasonable guesses of measurements.

gravity: a downward force that acts on objects near the surface of a planet or a moon.

height: the measurement of how tall something is.

length: the measurement of an object's longer side.

mass: the amount of matter in an object.

meter (m): basic metric unit of measurement used to measure length.

metric system: a system of weights and measures based on multiples of 10.

precise: exact.

temperature: a measure of how hot or cold something is.

thermometer: a tool for measuring temperature.

units: set amounts used as standards for measuring.

US customary system: a system of weights and measures based on the human body.

volume: the amount of space an object takes up.

weight: the measurement of the pull of gravity on an object.

width: the measurement of an object's shorter side.

Further Reading

Adler, David A. 2017. *Let's Estimate: A Book About Estimating and Rounding Numbers.* New York: Holiday House.

Barner, Bob. 2017. *Ants Rule: The Long and Short of It.* New York: Holiday House.

Rustad, Martha E. H. 2019. *Measuring Temperature.* Measuring Masters. North Mankato, Minn.: Pebble.

Vogel, Julia. 2018. *Weight.* New York: AV2 by Weigl.

Additional Notes

The page references below provide answers to questions asked throughout the book. Questions whose answers will vary are not addressed.

Page 15: You can answer in minutes or seconds, or a combination of both.

Page 17: If you weigh 100 pounds on Earth, you would weigh about 17 pounds on the Moon.

Page 19: The US customary unit for weight is pounds (lbs).

Page 21: You might want to know a container's volume for many reasons, such as measuring liquids in recipes.

Page 22: The volume of the box is 3,600 cm^3.

Page 25: Caption question: 80°F is about 26°C.

Index